GRADE 2

The Syllabus of Examinations should be read for details of requirements, especially those for scales, aural tests and sight-reading. Attention should be paid to the Special Notices on the inside front cover, where warning is given of any changes.

The syllabus is obtainable from music retailers or from The Associated Board of the Royal Schools of Music, 24 Portland Place, London W1B 1LU (please send a stamped addressed C5 (162mm × 229mm) envelope).

In examination centres outside the UK, information and syllabuses may be obtained from the Local Representative.

CONTENTS

Where appropriate, pieces in this volume have been checked with original source material and edited as necessary for instructional purposes. Fingering, phrasing, bowing, metronome marks and the editorial realization of ornaments (where given) are for guidance but are not comprehensive or obligatory.

DO NOT PHOTOCOPY © MUSIC

Alternative pieces for this grade

Music origination by Jack Thompson.
Cover by Økvik Design.
Printed in England by Halstan & Co. Ltd, Amersham, Bucks.

Fain would I wed

Arranged by
Edward Huws Jones

CAMPION

Fain would I wed is from Thomas Campion's *Fourth Booke of Ayres* published in 1617 or 1618. The melody is based on a popular chord sequence known as the 'passamezzo antico' – also found in *Greensleeves*. EHJ

Largo in D

Third Movement from Sonata in B minor, Op. 2 No. 7

Edited by
Richard Jones

PEPUSCH

The violin part, which is akin to a slow, stately dance tune, contrasts with the continuous tread of the 'walking-bass' accompaniment. The piece should be taken broadly, with generally long bow-strokes and expressive shaping of the phrases. Bowing (apart from that in bar 12), dynamics and articulation marks are editorial suggestions only.

Source: *Sonates à un violon seul & une basse continue*, Op. 2 (Amsterdam, 1707–8).

A:3

Gavotte

from *The Fashionable Dilettante Damon*

Transcribed and edited by
Richard Jones

TELEMANN

Fine

TRIO

D. C. al Fine

This is a shepherd's dance from Telemann's pastoral opera *Der neumodische Liebhaber Damon* (*The Fashionable Dilettante Damon*), which was first performed in Hamburg in 1724. The Gavotte was originally written for strings and the Trio for wind instruments. All dynamics and articulation marks are editorial suggestions only; the trill in bar 31 has also been added by the editor. In the original there is a trill in the melody on the first beat of bar 18.

Andantino in G

No. 4 from *Very Easy Melodious Exercises in the First Position*, Op. 22

B:1

ELGAR

This lovely melody needs a real sense of movement. The tempo must not be too slow or the bow can easily lose its flowing quality.

Reproduced by permission of Bosworth & Co. Ltd.
All enquiries for this piece apart from the examinations should be addressed to Bosworth & Co. Ltd, 8/9 Frith Street, London W1D 3JB.

B:2

Pastorale

NEGELY

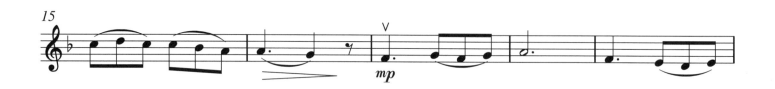

Reproduced from *The Young Violinist's Repertoire*, Book 2 by permission. All enquiries for this piece apart from the examinations should be addressed to Faber Music Ltd, 3 Queen Square, London WC1N 3AU.

Ancient Dance

B:3

LIUBOVSKI

© Copyright by Anglo-Soviet Music Press Ltd
Reproduced by permission of Boosey & Hawkes Music Publishers Ltd. All enquiries for this piece apart from the examinations should be addressed to Boosey & Hawkes Music Publishers Ltd, 295 Regent Street, London W1B 2JH.

AB 2746

A Quiet Conversation

No. 4 from *Up Bow, Down Bow*

RICHARD RODNEY BENNETT

Reproduced by permission of Novello & Co. Ltd.
All enquiries for this piece apart from the examinations should be addressed to Novello & Co. Ltd, 8/9 Frith Street, London W1D 3JB.

Coconuts and Mangoes

No. 14 from *Shooting Stars*

KATHERINE and
HUGH COLLEDGE

Jig

No. 3 from Little Suite No. 4

PETER MARTIN

Reproduced by permission. All enquiries for this piece apart from the examinations should be addressed to Stainer & Bell Ltd, PO Box 110, Victoria House, 23 Gruneisen Road, London N3 1DZ.

Checklist of Scales and Arpeggios

Candidates and teachers may find this checklist useful in learning the requirements of the grade. Full details of the forms of the various requirements, including details of rhythms, starting notes and bowing patterns, are given in the syllabus and in the scale books published by the Board.

Grade 2

			separate bows					slurred					
								two quavers to a bow					
Major Scales	C Major	1 Octave											
	F Major	1 Octave											
	G Major	2 Octaves											
	A Major	2 Octaves											
	B♭ Major	2 Octaves											
Minor Scales (*melodic* or *harmonic*)	G Minor	1 Octave						*two quavers to a bow*					
	D Minor	1 Octave											
	A Minor	1 Octave											
Major Arpeggios	C Major	1 Octave						*not applicable*					
	F Major	1 Octave											
	G Major	2 Octaves											
	A Major	2 Octaves											
	B♭ Major	2 Octaves											
Minor Arpeggios	G Minor	1 Octave						*not applicable*					
	D Minor	1 Octave											
	A Minor	1 Octave											